I0434591

MEN ARE DAWGS

By Eddie Burley

MEN ARE DAWGS

WARNING:

Unfortunately, most of the stories that you are about to read are true. The names have been changed to protect the guilty.

ABOUT THE AUTHOR

The author is an engineer from Atlanta who at an early age had his career and lifestyle altered due to a catastrophic spinal cord injury. Unable to further pursue his lifelong ambition in his chosen field, he became a self-taught computer technician and repairman. Refusing to be held down by life's obstacles, Mr. Burley authored his first book **'Handicap and loving it'**, where he uses his personal learning's and experiences as motivational tools in an attempt to help others.

'Handicap and loving it' - :
http://www.1stbooks.com/bookview/6317

ABOUT THE BOOK

'Men are dawgs' takes a look at one of life's issues from a different viewpoint. A view that people seldom want to discuss, is often overlooked, and very rarely acknowledged. Here the author attempts to bridge the gap of misunderstandings between men and women by displaying relationships from a man's point of view.

This is a story of atonement. About making amends with yourself, the world, and anyone that you've wronged before. This is a book requiring honesty. A reflective look in the mirror where one must examine and come to grips with who they truly are.

This book uses a series of short stories and exerts to depict different relationship situations for your reading entertainment.

MEN ARE DAWGS

By Eddie Burley

TABLE OF CONTENT

TITLE

MEN ARE DAWGS

By Eddie Burley

INTRODUCTION

CYCLES AND SALVATION

It was hard going through relationships. Repeatedly the results were the same. Relationships had proved convincingly that the odds of winning the lottery were better than finding the right mate. However, that suggestion just somehow didn't sound practical.

Something was very wrong, but the menacing culprit would not reveal it. Therefore, the decision was to examine the problem from within.

Analyzing situations from birth to present supplied ample ammunition to work with. Education, personal experiences, and research provided even more.

When all the considerations were examined and revealed, it became apparent that mans actions stood in direct correlations to situation in which he had been exposed.

MEN ARE DAWGS

By Eddie Burley

PREFACE

They are often liars, cheaters, and deceivers. Their behavior is sometimes low down, dirty, and despicable. Many times they can't be trusted and are manipulating devils. However, they are charming and charismatic. In addition to these descriptions one must include conniving, scornful, vengeful, and self-serving.

You never want to turn your back on them. At the same time, there is this magic. Something keeps drawing you back to them. Maybe, it's the superior intellect on their part. Perhaps it's the stupidity on your part. It may just be a combination of the two. Whatever it is, it's powerful enough to destroy lives, to change destinies, and to make submissive the most powerful forces known to mankind.

You can't live with them, and you sure as hell can't live without them.

MEN ARE DAWGS

By Eddie Burley

BIRTH OF A NOTION

This glorious morning mom was greeted to the birth of her fourth child. This would be her first and only bouncing baby boy.

"He's so beautiful," blurted the proud mother to her girlfriend. "He's going to be a heart throb and women are going to love him." "You'll see, I'm going to teach him how to be a *__"real man"__* and all about women so those little girls don't try to get over on my baby," Louise remarked, "cause child, woman are no good and you and I both know that." "Besides, there's not a woman out there good enough for my baby anyway." she added.

Her girlfriend Thelma nodded her head in agreement and said, "Honey, you know you're right. I try to teach my sons all about women's little tricks, but sometimes that don't even help," she added. "After all there was Adam and Eve," Thelma referenced. "If you face the facts the power of God was removed from the hands of man and placed in the hands of a woman all because of deceitfulness. How else could woman have become known as the mother of creation when she herself was created from the rib of a man," she chuckled.

ADAM AND EVETTE

IN THE BEGINNING, God created the heavens and the earth, and all was good. Then He created man in His own image.

Poor Adam was sitting around the crib one Sunday drinking a beer and watching football on his big screen TV, minding his own business, when Evette comes in and starts to bother him.

"Yo! Adam," she calls. "Woman, didn't I tell you don't be bothering me when I'm watching TV." he replies. "Oh, Adam, put down that remote control and come on over here to the Garden of Eden. I want to show you something."

"What, woman?" he ranged out. "Didn't God tell you to stay out of there and leave that stuff alone?" "Ahh, boy, you just scared, ya big sissy! Come on, it won't take long and then you can go right back. I promise. Please-e-e."

"All right, 5 minutes, but that's It." he barked. This was history's first recorded account of the 'quickie'.

Reluctantly, he gets up and strolls on over, still looking back trying to get a final glimpse at the score when Evette grabs him by his hand, rubs it up between her legs and says, "Here big boy, taste _this_ fruit."

You see the results; man has been screwed up ever since. Hell, he was still trying to recover from the fact that he had to give up a rib for her butt in the first place, and now this. Darn!

"Adam", God called. *"Adam, where art thou?"* came again the thunderous sound. "Oh, shoot," gestured Adam, "here comes da man!" "Don't be scared, gone out there," Evette edged him. *"Adam, why do you hide from me? Come on over here so I can ... holy cow. What happened to you Adam? Didn't I tell you not to eat the fruit from that garden?"* " Nah, Lord, see, I was running trying to come and see what you wanted and I pricked myself on that thorny bush over there and it just swelled up like this. I swear." Adam baffled. *"Thou shalt not lie,"* God commanded.

"Gone and tell him Adam, you ain't gotta be scared of him, you can make life too" added in Evette. "Yeah, that's right God, I gave him something that you couldn't."

God was furious.

Good thing Evette ducked that lightning bolt when she did or He would have split her again.

"Adam ... since you choose to obey woman instead of me, then this will be your fate forever more." God demanded.

Adam had really stepped in it now, knee deep in

poop. Lost a rib, lost the salvation of all mankind, and missed the end of the football game and he hadn't even been on the earth a week yet. He was having a bad day.

"And you," He said with a pause, now turning His attention to Evette as she tried to cowardly hide herself behind the fig leafs.

"That seed that you planted in your garden, you must now carry until maturity and then pass it through your womanhood as a reminder of your disobedience to God." He lashed out.

MOTHERS DON'T LIE,
(they just don't tell the truth)

Interestingly enough, men are birthed by women. This mere fact puts a man's faith solely in that woman's control and at the mercy of her disposal.

During the period of pregnancy, a child forms a bond with its mother. Dependency, reliability, comfort, and security all become influencing entities.

As an infant, a child relies on its mother again for food, nurturing, shelter, security, comfort, and etcetera.

Reliability, dependency, and loyalties are deeply embedded into this child's life. A child first learns everything from its mother. Even some of the earlier nursery rhymes lend credence to a progressive process of mind control to female domination. One such being, *'little girl's are made of sugar and spice and everything nice.'* Early learning also teaches idealistic views such as 'ladies first.' Teachings such as these can easily become very dangerous tools of exploitation in the wrong hands.

The bond that is made during this period will last a lifetime and its teachings will play an important role in a person's outcome and future.

This child will also bond with its father, siblings, and eventually other people. However, each bond will occur on a different level, none of which will come close in comparison to that of its mother. Mom's guidance and teachings will affect the degree of the level for all other bonds that follows.

If this family structure is congealing, chances are good that a child's nurturing and rearing will be well balanced. However, the mothers influence remains the determining principle. This exists because mothers often make children feel obligated or guilty for the period of pregnancy with statements such as, 'I carried you for nine months.'

Moms teaching and influences are based primarily on that mother's personal life experiences and desires. It is important to remember, that every mother, was once one of those women that your child will grow up to meet.

Hilariously, women have the audacity to say that they will teach their sons to be a man, one part of life in which they have absolutely no experience. Women have the audacity to say that a man has potential but just needs to be 'trained' or 'groomed.' In actuality, what they really mean is that he needs to be fine-tuned with that woman's personal influence to meet her particular needs and hope.

What a woman fails to realize though, is that one must be careful of what they ask for. After her son reaches adulthood and began gaining knowledge from his own life experiences, he begins to realize that life does not quite compare to the normalcy of his mother's expectations or teachings. Consequently, he, like any being, rejects abuse and the thought of being conquered. He becomes like a wounded or caged animal. Naturally, he strikes out and fights back seeking to find his own way, independence, and freedom from the chains that bound him. Of course, this action then becomes misconstrued as not being a good man or a 'dawg. However, one must consider the source and by whose standards this judgment is being made.

With a lifetime of emotions and loyalties that it took to form these bonds, no one really wants to admit or accept the fact that their mothers teaching may have been somewhat tainted. Whether it was done consciously or unconsciously, its deception is still paramount to that of a lie.

THREE LITTLE PIGGIES

Once upon a time, there were three little piggies. There was a Vivian pig, a Terri pig, and a Catherine pig. These piggies all had something in common. They each had a baby by a man named Eric. Eric loved them each, individually, at different intervals in his life.

The Vivian pig and Eric grew up as childhood friends. They played and went to school together. A period passed in life when they each went their own separate ways. One day after a long absence, they bumped into each other. Jubilations were in the air at a chance to see an old friend again.

Eric and Vivian began spending lots of time together. They vowed never to make distance between two friends a problem again. They talked about the old times and they talked about the future. They never talked about each other. Even though Eric had a childhood crush on her all his life, he dared not chance to jeopardize his friendship.

During one of Eric's departures, Vivian asked him for a favor. He felt honored to be able to oblige. "Kiss me," Vivian requested. Stunned, Eric reached over and kissed her on the forehead. "Not like that," Vivian said disappointedly, "I want a real kiss," she demands.

The kiss went better than expected. After

catching their breath, they kissed again, and again, and again. Needless to say, they were no longer *'just friends.'*

Vivian told Eric that she was pregnant one day, when in reality she was not. Eric was ecstatic, so he asked Vivian to marry him. Later, she told him the truth, but that truth put a strain on their relationship. Months later, Vivian was pregnant for true. This time Eric didn't believe her. Vivian wanted to marry, but Eric said no. He didn't feel that he could trust her anymore.

Vivian put Eric up for child support and moved far, far away so he could never see his child again.

When the child turned 18, he left Vivian and went to live with Eric. To this date, Vivian lives alone in seclusion, with no Eric, no child, and no child support checks.

Eric met the Terri pig in a nightclub. Terri was a fun person to be with, but full of mischief. For some reason though, they worked well together. Eric raised her standards of living immensely after their baby was born. However, Terri was not a very responsible person.

They argued and fought often. Soon their run ended. Terri marveled in delight at the amount of child support that she received. Eric moved on.

One day at work, Eric met the Catherine pig. There was no special relationship there, but they were a little bit more than friends. They had three children together in their tenure. The problem though, was that Catherine wanted to take everything from the relationship but not put anything in.

She would later take the household furnishings and her child support checks and then she parted company.

Eric one day had an accident. He was no longer able to work. All the healthy child support payments that he was responsible for paying had now been reduced to mere social security payments. Terri pig and Catherine pig were outraged. "My hair and nails need to be done," Terri squawked. "My car note is due," shouted Catherine. No one was concerned about the state of Eric's condition, only that of his bank account.

No one had anymore necessity for Eric since his finances were exacerbated. Alone they all left him with no help and deep in debt.

Although the situation seemed bleak, Eric found a sigh of relief in it all. He was no longer being gnawed on by the piggies.

Eric began to claw his way back out of the hole as the piggies set back and watched with laughter. "Poor old fool, why don't he just give up and die," they clattered. Eric was not about to quit.

Then one day, Eric's long time friend, Emily, appeared on the scene. The piggies saw her coming but they didn't take her seriously, probably just out of disrespect. Well, Emily didn't fret that any. "That poor old man, he sure could use some help," Emily thought to herself, and so help him she did.

The piggies were hot enough to stew in their own sauces. "Oh, naw she didn't," squealed the Catherine pig. "Who does she think that she is, moving into my house," she brewed. "Watch and see, I'm going to break that mess up," ushered in Terri.

These piggies tried for a very long time to come between things with Eric and Emily. They used every trick in the book. They even worked together at times. They huff and they puffed, but they couldn't blow Eric's house down.

Eric and Emily went on to get married and they lived happily ever after.

SERVING TWO MASTERS

Grandmas are great. Suppose after years of causing their share of pain and torment to others, guilt sets in and they feel a sense of responsibility to their grandsons. Grandmas always spew out words of wisdom, one being, "be careful out there, women will chase you until you catch them."

Many years of trials and tribulations will pass before any of these words collectively began to make any sense.

You see, grandmas know that men have a problem. It's rather hard to explain and actually there's no place to lay the blame. It is perhaps the result of some genetically mishap or something.

Man, is the most dominant and intelligent living being on the face of the earth. He conquers all. He holds the most prestigious, and mind boggling jobs that we as humans have to offer.

There is one small problem though; 'sex.' Sex is great, and it's a very necessary function in nature to continue and ensure the regeneration of a species. Birds do it. Bees do it, and we do it. However, in every other species of life there is a designated copulation by design.

Flowers pollinate in the spring. Salmon's do their spawning at the end of summer and etcetera.

One of man's unique and distinct characteristics lies in the fact that he is capable of sex the entire year round. Another grave distinction is that unlike all other forms of life that indulge in sex as a process of life's cycle, man on the other hand will indulge in sex merely for pleasure.

At first glance, this seems like an excellent benefit to being a man. Mind you, granny also said, "every advantage has a disadvantage." Man has two major organs, of which are dominating and formidable forces to be reckoned with. That would be his brain and his genitals. Both of these organs are often commonly referred to as 'head.' In order for either 'head' to perform at the maximum of its capacity, the body must supply that organ with a large amount of blood. Herein lays the problem. The body cannot supply sufficient quantities of blood to both heads simultaneously. This is a result of that genetic flaw. When a man is thinking well, he's not having sex. So obviously, when he's having sex, then he's not thinking well.

Down time of either head leaves a man gullible and these gullibility's are considered as a weakness. Hence, when a man is involved with a woman, he is often apt not to make good decisions. These periods of poor decision-making are frequently confused as stupidity.

Grandmas also say, "All that glitters ain't gold." When the blood is above a man's shoulders, he can deal with a bad situation in a manor that is contusive to good civil liberties. Given; any time during that bad situation if a woman turns on her feminine charms, the blood will drop below the belt. At this point, you may as well throw caution in the wind.

When he loses his thoughts and goes for that 'fool's gold', she now has him in a very vulnerable position of which you can be sure that she will take full advantage of.

SAMPSON AND DELILAH SON

A long time ago, on one of the beaches in southern California, this scrawny little kid named Sampson laid playing in the sand. Out of nowhere came a group of thugs who kicked sand in his face and pushed his little castle down. While lying there in despair, a sudden gust of wind blew debris across his path.

An ad on the back of a comic book cover happened to catch his eye. It read; *'Tired of being pushed around on the beach by bullies? Well, you too can become a super hero and run those bullies away. Send your check or money order to the address below and get started today. Sorry, no C.O.D.'*

By God, Sampson jumped to his feet and ran home in a heated rush. Once inside he climbed the stairs to his room and broke open his piggy bank jar. Counted out the money as required by the ad and his order was off.

Two days later his package had arrived for he placed his order using overnight express. Little Sampson wasted no time tearing into that package. He grabbed out his bottle of pills, popped two in his mouth, and swallowed them down without hesitation. Almost instantly, he could feel that his body was about to change. He could feel the power in his muscles when his strength began to develop and his arm sizes grew. Immediately, Sampson popped down a couple more pills.

Then he read the accompanying pamphlet to find out more about them. The label on the side of the bottle went as follows: '*WARNING: Mild side affects could occur with some users, extreme hair growth, nausea, or diarrhea. To reverse the affect of this drug, simply cut hair from the head. If problem persist more than 10 days consult a physician. KEEP OUT OF THE REACH OF CHILDREN.*'

Sampson felt good about himself and day-by-day his self-esteem grew. People in the neighborhood began noticing him too. They admired his gentle spirit and hard work ethics. As he walked down the street, locals in the area would shout out to him, "Yo' Sampson, looking good ése." One could always count on Sampson for help, as by now his strength was legendary. There was a time when his neighbor's car skidded off the road and went down an embankment. No problem for Sampson, he climbed down the side of the hill, and pushed his friend back to safety without breaking a sweat. The people of the area knew that they could always count on Sampson.

Alas, as all good stories go, peace would not last long for this quaint little village. From the east coast came a group of thugs who unleash a rein of terror amongst the local population. The villagers got word out to Sampson. There was never any doubt that he'd be able to handle this situation.

Sampson made light work of this group. The locals cheered from afar while the thugs retreated over the hill. This joy would be short lived however. The west coast had experienced thugs before, but never anything like these guys from the east. These guys where not easily deterred. They'd set out attacks on the village repeatedly and each time Sampson would turn them away.

During one of his defenses of the town, Sampson saw a beautiful damsel in distress named Delilah Son. Delilah Son's kitten was stuck in a tree when Sampson, her savior and hero happened to be passing by. After he rescued her cat, they chatted and exchanged phone numbers. Later they strolled down to the local bistro for a cup of cappuccino.

It was love at first sight for Sampson and his eyes were all aglow but for Delilah Son the feelings were not quiet the same. During one of their outings on the town, the thugs returned. Young Sampson kicked butt as he had so many times before. These guys desperately needed to find a way to defeat Mr. Sampson. On the other hand, Delilah Son was a very opportunistic person. She knew that if she could find the secret to Sampson's strength, that she could line her pockets with gold.

Well, Delilah Son made several assassination attempts on young Sampson's life. She laced his meal with enough poison to wipe out a small village, but Sampson asked for a second serving. She thrusted a dagger deep into his back and he never even twitched. Then Delilah Son even wired explosives to his chariot and ruined a great set of rims. Once more, Sampson left unharmed. Delilah Son had noticed though how giddy Samson would be every time he was in her presence.

Sampson came over one afternoon to pick Delilah Son up for lunch. This day she decided to hit him with that 'peal (sex appeal).

Delilah Son came down the stairs with tassels on her nipples, a black leather g-string, and black stiletto pumps. Naturally, Sampson rose to the occasion.

Unfortunately for Sampson, all the blood had left his head to go down south. Now, with an unclear mind, Delilah Son was able to coerce Sampson to reveal the secret of his strength. Then he smoked a cigarette and went to sleep.

In this vulnerable state, Delilah Son gently clipped the locks of hair from Sampson's head. With his strength neutralized, she sold this information to the thugs for a pot of gold.

Sampson awoke to find himself surrounded by the gang. Not yet realizing that his hair was gone, he jumped up to commence kicking tail as he had so many times before. The gang beat Sampson down severely. So, therefore, goes another saga in the downfall of man.

HOUSEWIVES AND HOES

Taking in consideration the honesty and the fee, marriage and prostitution are very similar. They are both forms of gold digging. Of the two prospective, though, prostitution happens to be the most honest form of a relationship or lack there-of.

Hoes are actually more respectable because of their honesty. Right from the start, you know that there is no lasting relationship. You know how much money it is going to cost for sex and exactly what you will get for the money you spend. When your money is gone, then she is too. She is probably coming to you right after providing the same service for another man and she is probably going to another man as soon as she leaves you.

This prostitute will bring to you no tricks, lies, manipulation, or deception. She will bring you no babies that may or not be yours. Every time you meet her, she will exploit her attractive and feministic side. You will never see any hair rollers in this woman's head.

There will be no arguments and she will never turn her back to you talking about she has a headache tonight. There is no mother-in-law to butt into one's affairs. There are also no lazy relatives who may need to borrow money from you, or occasionally need a place to stay.

These women will never reject you and you will never hear them say 'no.'

Any fantasy or desire you possess will be fulfilled. You can have as many women as you want for as many times as you want. All you need to bring to the table is the libido and the cash. You never have to see the same woman twice and when you are done with that woman, you're done.

Once this woman applies the skills of her trade, your pleasure and satisfaction takes center stage on a list of her agendas. You can beat your last dollar, which is probably what it's going to take, that by the time this woman has finished with you that you both are completely satisfied. That helps to account for why prostitution is one of the oldest profession in the world.

Housewives on the other hand, are still prostitutes, just on a different level. Instead of seeking out the pleasure that you desire, you become the seeked.

Regardless to how enviable this position seems the consequences are costly.

Women seek out marriage perspectives based on two important relative factors: (1) Financial worth and (2) Financial potential. Now, they are going to tell you how much they love you and the one about 'you're the only man for me.' In addition, without a doubt she'll spend a little bit more time with you in an effort to occupy a space in your life and keep your interest in your initial investment. Nevertheless, what they actually mean is that 'I found gold here and I'm about to fight like hell to maintain my stake on this claim. Any denials to this statement could easily be resolved with the signing of a prenuptial agreement that contains a no alimony or property settlement clause. Fare warning though, that suggestion is going to cost you like hell.

There exists the possibility that the wedding will be called off and the sum of your total investments will be lost. Alternatively, you could become the victim of a guilt trip for even suggesting such a practical idea. Well, this display of rationality will cost your original down payment to more than double trying to apologize and prove your sense of trustworthiness to an untrustworthy person.

Now you're a victim of manipulation and deceit. So there you are apologizing and paying for being screwed (literarily speaking). What is even worst, you haven't even gotten married yet.

Contrary to popular believe, the quality of the sex don't necessarily improve because you pay more for it. Interestingly enough you begin by paying for your sex in advance. This works as a lay-a-way plan, if you will. The initial down payment consists of wining and dining, flowers and jewelry, and finally the cost of a wedding or funeral, as it will eventually turn out to be.

Right after you've swallowed a good dose of 'hooked, hog tied, and sinker,' there'll come a morning when you wake to find out that your 'belle of the ball' has turned out to be your 'ball and chain.' You just went from being screwed literally to being screwed financially and your wife has had a headache for the last six months.

Go right ahead, head for that door if you want to. Just on, the other side is a divorce lawyer with alimony papers and a pen, saying "sign here." So true it is that she had nothing when you met her. The problem is you've raised her lifestyle and standards of living. Now you must provide to maintain that standard, even though you are leaving.

Women are quick though; one more psychological ploy is about to go upside your head. "Gold digging, ha, you don't have anything to take." she'll reply.

Don't go for it. The free shelter, the shopping sprees, dinners on the town, your work benefits, and alimony payments will do fine for starters. Moreover, heaven forbid if you where unfortunate enough to have kids. You have now become the proud owner of 'not a darn thing.' Everything that was once yours is now hers. To add insult to injury, you'll have to keep throwing good money after bad until the last child turns 18 years of age.

Oh yeah, remember how that prostitute heads to the arms of another man after she's done with you, well, guess where this one's going.

Although there is a variation in the paths of the road that's traveled, the destination remains the same, women trading sex for money. Ironically, the major difference between the two is that women of marriage seek to desecrate and perform character assassination against women of prostitution in an effort to thwart off the competition. In essence though, they are performing the same service. Women of marriage merely attempt to par lee their payments into a high stake wager seeking to multiply their earnings while constantly reducing the services that they provided.

PROUD MARY

Okay, now there was this little girl named Mary, and she was married to some old fart named Joseph. Joseph was a shepherd you know. It wasn't as if you had much of a choice of too many jobs back in the days. You could be a shepherd, a carpenter, or a slave. Pretty much the same as it is today.

Joseph and Mary had been having problems in the 'sac'. They try to say it was because he was sterile, yet, he end up begetting a baby later on in the story.

Word around town was that he had erectile dysfunction. All he had to do was go down and talk to his doctor about it. Nah, they didn't have Viagra just yet, but still he could have grind up some herbs and roots in one of those medicine bowls. Boiled it up like a tea, and drank the hot broth off the top, or something like that.

Hell, they were parting the Red Sea and turning staffs into snakes back then, so surely they could have made a penis stand up.

Now Mary, I understand had a little 'back' on her. She was supposed to be pretty 'fly' too. Besides, she was a very proud woman, that's why people in the 'hood called her 'Proud Mary'.

I don't know how you look at it, but, the way I see it, Mary had been creeping. Now, Joseph can't get it up, she goes to sleep one night and wake up the next day pregnant, "hello!" Well, she drove down to the corner market there to get one of those early pregnancy test things; you know the kind that tells you when you're pregnant. As you know by now, it came back positive.

You ever notice that you don't see too many pictures of Joseph and especially with Mary. Even when you do see him, it's in a dark or cloudy looking setting. Well, that's because Joseph had some 'brother' in him. When he found out that Mary was pregnant, the first word out of his mouth was, "Witch!", but with a "B".

Well, I guess you know it wasn't long before the neighbors started talking. People would laugh at Joseph when his back was turned. Nevertheless, often they would try to hit up on Mary when he wasn't around.

He even thought about leaving her butt for a while there. Hell, nobody was buying that stuff about getting pregnant and not screwing. Joseph started going 'off' on her. She had brought shame and humiliation upon this household. Baby Jesus and Mary were about to get their holy butts whopped.

The scene was getting ugly here. Mobs were forming to stone her to death for most people liked old Joseph. God had to do something to squash this noise and protect His unborn son. Well, He pulled old Joseph over to the side and broke him off on a little piece of action for later on down the line. If Mary hadn't been wearing that sexy underwear from Victoria's Secret that night then baby Jesus might not have ever been born. Let me tell you that must have been some 'Holy Night.'

God had Joseph to go out, talk to the people, and tell them he had a vision where God had spoken to him. People liked and respected Joseph so they weren't gonna doubt his word too much. Therefore, since most people were peasants and not very educated, God and Joseph come up with a big ol' long word that nobody quite knew the meaning of called 'immaculate conception'.

All right, so the people bought it, besides it had certain rings of omnipotence about it. Now just because the people weren't educated it sure as hell didn't mean that they were stupid either. People watch stuff, and if they like it, they copy it and try it. Before you know it, people were screwing everywhere. So when the babies turned up that obviously weren't the fathers, the first thing the woman would say was, "God gave me this baby." Hell, it was so effective until women still try to use it today.

Good thing that new d.n.a. stuff is out now; it stops a whole bunch of lies.

On the other hand, on the other side of the fence, men found certain benefits in it to. They saw God drop off a baby for Joseph to take care of so other men started doing the same. Besides, they were made in the same image. It worked out pretty good there for a long time, too. Only now, they call that being a 'dead-beat dad', and they make your butt pay child support, too.

CAN'T FIND A GOOD MAN

An often-made complaint about men is that it's hard to find a good one. Hard to find a compatible one would more justly describe the situation, but to say a 'good' one, well, that's a little far fetched.

A man's character has always consisted of certain things; God fearing, loyalty, and obedience, even when the odds are stacked deep against him. Corruption, manipulation, and deceit are a few obstacles that are often thrown into his path in an attempt to stray his course. However, in being true to his inner self, his strengths will help him to stay 'par for the course.'

First, it's very hard to believe that there is not some good in everyone. Second, it's just as inconceivable to believe that nearly every man a woman meets is bad. When a relationship don't quiet pan out the way one expects, it doesn't mean that the whole gender is bad. It merely means that that was not the right scenario for you. In these cases, a woman should call on one of her skills in an area in which she has plenty of experience, 'shopping.'

For instance, if a woman sees this cute little pair of shoes that she feels she absolutely must have, she will go look at them, check the price, and try them on.

They'll compare them with other styles,

different colors, and in different sizes until they find something that's comfortable. Then they'll check the price again. Next, she'll shop their compatibility with hats, belts, pants, dresses, and etcetera.

From there, she'll shop other department stores for savings, bargains, sales, and compatibility.

By the time this process is complete, she'll probably have bought nothing.

Other women will shop and choose a shoe that is very unbecoming of them. It may not be the right size or color but they'll take it anyway. Later on after a few bunions or sore foot pains, they'll be mad at the designer or the shoe store. This is all because they tried to stick a big fat foot into a half size smaller shoe.

The real side of the story is a failure to select quality and pay attention to detail. Relationships are not that much different. In order to give a relationship a better chance to survive one should be as selective in love as in shopping, or you should be prepared for bunions.

Women often try to stick a square peg into a round whole. They seem to buy into that misconception that opposites attract. Women don't necessarily make the best decisions when selecting a mate. A church girl chooses a bad boy. A schoolteacher chooses a drug dealer, and the mismatches continue. There are a number of reasons for these choices. Maybe it's the way he walks, the way he talks, or just the way he looks. It may even just be because he's with another woman that she despise. Nine out of ten qualifying conditions could be wrong in selecting this mate, but she'll select him anyway. Why, because women believe they can change a man's attitude, personality, or style with her sex. This is sometimes called grooming, training, fine-tuning, and a list of other names. The short of it is though it doesn't work.

True, he may be susceptible to compromise and adapt to new changes for a while or give in to a certain point, but the woman's control begins to try to dominate.

She will never be satisfied or appreciate the changes that have been made. She will constantly push for more changes until the man's personality and identity has been lost and he becomes uncomfortable. Whoa! Houston, we have a problem. Now you're trying to get this bad boy, who was totally out of character for you in the first place to now be a choirboy. Ladies, it's not going to happen. He's going to reject everything that you tried to institute. He's going to resent you for trying to make him change. Not only will he resort back to the personality that you found so interesting in the first place, but he may add a few additional changes of his own that you just absolutely can not stand.

Well guess what ladies, now you have a bunion and you want to blame the shoe store or designer for trying to stick your big fat foot into that tiny little shoe.

NOAH'S HOOPTY

Over a period of years after Evette had unleashed this terrible fiasco unto the world, the new offspring's grew. Their hormones hit a fevered pitch too. Brothers started doing sisters, brothers started doing brothers, and brothers were even doing the sheep. Sisters often laid with dogs and frequently found themselves fascinated with how well endowed the horses were hung.

There was incest, homosexuality, drug abuse, and drunkenness everywhere. The party was 'on' ya'll. The whole world was just one big orgy.

The Lord wasn't doing too well at recruiting new members' right about this point. This 'creation' thing was getting a lot tougher than it first seemed. Oh yeah, sure, the flowers, trees, air, water, and things like that were a piece of cake. That was not a problem. Now, having to deal with a hardheaded woman, hell, who would have thought it, could be so difficult.

Any ways, the Lord started contemplating ways how best to correct these wrongs. He didn't want to just scrap the whole thing for the world was still a good idea to have. Besides a lot of good work had gone into this thing. **"Seems like it still has a pretty good chance of working,"** the Lord thought. **"If only there was some way I could wash there sins away."** He pondered.

"That's it! I'll just wash them off the face of the earth. How long could that take?" He exclaimed!

So now as the Lord returned to do His work, He happened to notice the message light was 'on' on His answering machine. It was Noah again, calling the Lord trying to figure out what to do next. Noah was a meek man, not very good with the ladies and incapable of making decisions on his own, but he was a good carpenter. **"Oh, Noah, with all I have to do you call me everyday"**, the thoughts pass in His mind. He knew it was Noah before he even checked His messages because Noah was the <u>only</u> one who ever called Him anyway. **"Hmmm, maybe you're worth saving too."** God jested.

"Noah", the Lord called. Noah froze in his tracks and began to look around. **"Noah"**, God called out again. This time Noah took off and ran. Here we go again, the Lord must have thought. Therefore, He called once more but this time with the deafening force of thunder. ***"Noah"***, He said.

Noah immediately stopped and dropped to his knees. Some say that it was because he was in the presence of the Lord. Others say it was because the event scared him so bad that he lost control of his bowels. Suppose we'll never really know for sure, because it was a long, long, long time ago.

The Lord proceeded to give Noah instruction about his task. Noah was expected to carry out every detail without wavering and without question.

Okay, so now here sits Noah, out in the middle of the desert building this big freaking ship. Nobody really paid him a lot attention at first for Noah always was a strange type of fellow of sorts.

Even his own family was going, "Yo mom, I think dad fell off the ladder one time too many."

Gradually the word started to get out about Noah and the crowds began to gather. People flocked in with amazement by the multitudes to see this spectacular phenomenon. Even Guinness was there with his record book. Noah was going to be the first man to make a ship sail on dry land.

Crowds began to form and they grew larger and larger. The ridicule started to pour in but Noah never stopped or strayed from his task at hand, neither did the partying either for that matter.

Then the day came upon when this behemoth of a vessel was near completion. The large crowds stood stunned and very awed with dismay when they realized that there were no luxury class seats or restroom accommodations aboard.

"I wouldn't sail on that ship with him if he was the last man on earth," one spectator shouted and the crowd jeered. How little did they know?

After a brief rest, the Lord spoke to Noah again, this time his instructions were simple. Go out, get a male and a female of every species, and bring them aboard the ark. The instructions were so simple that even a child could understand.

As Noah continued to herd, the last of his passengers aboard the ark the rain began to fall. The rain fell pretty much in a drizzle at first until Noah had all his passengers safely inside.

The crowds outside were taking wagers as to how far he was going to go. The odds were not in Noah's favor at this time.

Soon the thunderstorms and the rain clouds grew to a catastrophic proportion. Doppler radar issued tornado warnings for the immediate surrounding areas on CNN News Live with Connie Chung. African street vendors set up side walk stands selling Totes umbrellas and galoshes. Business was booming everywhere.

It must have rained like hell for about four or five days. Heavy high winds and gale thunderstorms rocked the boat savagely from side to side.

Bombardment after bombardment of hail the size of golf balls, pounded across the deck of this mammoth vessel sending echoes of fear through everyone and everything inside. Some of the vicious downpour of rains even found its way inside through cracks in Noah's armor.

Noah wrestled with himself unendingly about witnessing first hand the Lords work and the devastation of all mankind until finally curiosity got the best of him. He made his way around inside the belly of this giant ship, occasionally stepping in piles of animal droppings, until he reached a porthole window on the starboard side.

There he loosened the bindings that held a protective shield in place. Once this was removed, he took a chance to stick his head outside and see what was left of his home and his land.

When Noah's head appeared outside, the large crowds roared with laughter. The people were hysteric. Instant replays of the event were televised through out the land. Jay Leno even did a comic sketch on the Tonight Show.

By now God was going, **"Jumpin' Jehoshaphat Noah, it only took me 6 days to create this blessed thing!"**

Poor Noah, he really meant well, but he was just not one of the brightest bulbs in the lamp. He had actually used so much timber in the construction of the ark that the rainwater washed everything downhill together and formed a dam. This prevented the rainwater from ever reaching his vessel.

My friends, this is the reason that it took 40 days and 40 nights. However, Noah was a good man.

IF THE SHOE FITS

Dianne was a beautiful and intelligent woman and success had followed her through out her life. Because she held dominant positions in the work force, her combinations often left men intimidated. Her husband, Andy was a meek man. They married right out of high school and had been married for twenty-four years to this date. Over the years, he too became intimidated by Dianne because of her leadership roles. The last few years Dianne's health had left her unable to work.

Uneducated Andy could only hold down mediocre jobs and found it necessary to work two jobs just to make ends meet. Dianne had an appetite for the finer things in life that Andy could not provide. On previous occasions in the past, she'd managed to supplement her income by keeping the company of other male friends, unbeknown to her husband. However, this particular time she took on a part-time position as a property manager in order to help with their rent. The physical strain of the job and their financial wows left Dianne unable to keep up her appearance and very deeply depressed. She still managed though to impose an intimidating figure because of her position.

A time came at work when the job load was so

severe that she found it necessary to enlist the aide of an outside contractor. That's where Dave comes on the scene. He had come highly recommended through one of her employees. He ranked high as one of the leading contractors in his field. Dave was a married man. He too was highly educated and a very intimidating figure.

Although, he was a good-looking and masculine man, Dave was a roughneck. He liked his money, his liquor, and his women.

Dianne liked him immediately. He was very much a take-charge guy. He was fast to solve problems, which stopped complaints to the office thus taking pressure off her. They respected each other's positions and styles. An occurrence came about though, when Dianne made a mistake. She discussed Dave's financial arrangements in front of another employee.

"You talk too much," Dave blurted out with a stone cold look on his face. Dianne was speechless. She just stood there with her mouth hanging open. Everyone else cleared the area. No one knew what to expect next.

"Gee, that's the first time a man has ever talked to me like that before. You act as if you've known me all my life. I know I talk too much, but no man has ever said that to me before. I'm sorry Dave, I was wrong. I just didn't think," she said in an apology. "How can I make it up to you," Dianne added. "Have lunch with me," answered Dave. "I have no money," Dianne replied. "That's not what I asked you," he said. "Okay, just give me a few minutes," responded Dianne.

Lobster was her favorite food. After a couple of steaks and lobster, they each had several drinks. Then he told her that he had a crush on her. "That's the first time I've ever seen you smile," said Dave. "That's because lately I haven't had anything to smile about," replied Dianne as she began explaining her situation. She was impressed by his ability to have knowledgeable and intelligent conversations. However, she was even more impressed with his lack of fear for spending money.

One of Dianne's problems was a pass due debt. Dave peeled off the amount that she needed from a roll of money in his pocket and gave it to her. Dianne had been in affairs before so she agreed to meet with him later.

Back on the job, Dave was working in a vacant apartment unit. Dianne left her husband Andy at home to baby sit. She told him she needed to inspect the property. She entered the unit where Dave was working. He pulled her close to him by the belt buckle and began to unloose the snaps. "Oh, you turned me on when you did that," Dianne said as she removed the rest of her clothes. Then she walked over to the counter and leaned over now exposing herself to him. Dave wasted no time demonstrating to her his other many skills. He did things that her husband never dreamed of. He had little inhabitations and was as aggressive in his style of lovemaking as he was in his work.

This escapade went on for several months. Andy became suspicious because Dianne was once again increasing her appearance and having money to spend. He also noticed that she was spending more time with Dave. Andy wanted to confront Dave about it, but he was just no match physically, mentally, or financially, so he confronted Dianne instead. She told Andy all about the relationship and asked him to leave the home.

Rejected and broken hearted Andy saw no other recourse and so he did.

After twenty-four years of marriage, Dianne too was understandably upset with Andy's departure. Of her many extramarital affairs in the past, this is the first one that had ever been found out about.

Sobbing, she called Dave into the office. When he arrived, she told him what had occurred. He consoled her and then he made love to her. She was fine there for a while until it was time for him to go home.

"I'm afraid to stay here by myself tonight," she said crying. "Can't you please just spend one night with me? In the last twenty-four years, I have never had to be in the house alone whether we slept together or not.

Please."

Dave was hesitant because he knew that he too had a spouse at home. She pleaded with him more and reluctantly he agreed to stay. He later called his wife and told her that he would be working out of town for the evening.

That night they lay entangled in each other's arms, making love several times through out the night. The next morning Dianne had a startling revelation. "I felt so safe and secure sleeping in the arms of a strong man. It's as though nothing could ever harm me when I'm with you. Andy always turned the alarm on before he goes to bed and you say it makes you feel like you're in prison. I never felt this much freedom before," Dianne rambled like a schoolgirl. "Dave, I've been thinking," she continued, "Since I told Andy about us, you owe it to me to go home and tell your wife too. That way we won't have to continue to sneak around. What do you think?"

Dave stood there in silence glaring out the window. "Dave…Do you hear me Dave…Dave, say something," she urged. Dave just stood there. She walked over in front of where he stood and she could see tears rolling down his cheeks.

"Baby, what's wrong," she questioned. "I never meant for anyone to get hurt," he said with a trembling voice. "I guess I'm just not as strong as you. I can't leave my wife. She has nothing to do with this. She doesn't deserve to be hurt like this. I just can't do it. I'm sorry. I'm sorry."

"But Dave," Dianne pleaded, "I left my husband for you." "I know," answered Dave, "and that disturbs me too. "If you left him for me, then you may leave me for someone else. I just can't do it Dianne," he said before he left.

TWISTED SISTA

A male child born of the Caribbean's moved to this country seeking a better way of life along with his mother. Brought with him was his ability to prepare gourmet cuisines and a hard work ethnic.

Upon his arrival he landed a job at a major hotel as a Head Chef. In his first year there he was able to purchase a white Ford Bronco and a three bedroom home. His expectations were being met at a records pace.

Well, Rick one day met this ebony beauty queen. A queen for true she may not have been, but beautiful for sure she was. They began to see each other on a regular basis and soon became an item. Over a year or so later they were married and the proud parents of a newborn baby girl. Denise, Rick's new bride moved into the home that he and his mother had shared.

Dating someone and seeing them on a regular basis is much more different than seeing someone everyday, Rick soon found out. The time they spent together and the things they did before that she once appreciated were now being taken for granted. Denise had high maintenance expectations and totally rejected the idea of helping to contribute into the family upkeep. The next six months proved unbearable for the two.

Unable to work through their differences, Denise filed for divorce.

Denise was awarded alimony, child support, the car and the home in the settlement, while Rick and his mother was force to occupy a smaller two bedroom apartment elsewhere.

Fortunate for Rick his work ethic was strong. He went to school at night and learned a trade of Heating and Air Conditioning. Upon completion of his course he was able to take on a second job. In less than three months Rick put together enough monies for down payment and purchased another home for him and his mom.

Once Denise got a hold of that information she went back into the courts and had her payments increased. Increased so much, in fact, that she never had to work. Frustrating indeed this was for the man. However, he didn't have too much choice in the matter. There was the house note, the car payment, and a student loan due in order to preserve his good credit rating. Desperately needing money, Rick began doing extra jobs from his home. He'd earn money working on cars, repairing appliances, or whatever he could just to make ends meet. The man had two full time jobs and a hustle.

Unfortunately for Rick though, his reputation for quality and service preceded him. It wasn't long thereafter before Denise was back into the courts where she received yet another rate increase.

Already strapped for cash, Rick found himself at the losing end of a dilemma. He fought through it for almost a year just to find that he was falling further and further behind. With no other recourse in sight Rick sold his home and moved back to his native island.

Denise can now be found somewhere in Atlanta living with family where she receives food stamps and government assistance.

A CHEATING MAN

This person is not a monogamist in a relationship. The lack of monogamy is one of the major reasons for marital failures. To pull this act off, one must open up many other avenues. It's virtually the last piece to fall in a domino effect. First to fall is lying. There is a funny thing about lying. Lying takes on a completely new life of its own. To tell a person that you love them and then cheat on them is perhaps the greatest lie of all. Lies cut two ways. It violates the trust between you and your mate, and secondly, it perpetrates deceit and deception from the person telling the lie.

Honesty then becomes an issue in which time, money, possessions, and actions eventually will need to be accounted for. It order to account for them, one must institute cunning and even more lies. The more lies that are used in this deception, the harder it becomes to maintain a cover story. The harder the cover is the more flaws appear in the lies. After a succession of continuous flaws, then the trust is lost.

Once your trust is in jeopardy, you no longer have credibility. Then finally, without credibility, there is no respect.

The biggest thing that makes a man a cheater is his inability not to be caught. Women cheat often but are rarely found out about. They target men who are doing well by his lady. They target men out of spike for another woman. They target men who are completely opposite of their mate, and they target men just for fun.

Women are well aware of a mans potential to be a cheater because most of the women they are cheating with are cheaters themselves.

WHY DO MEN CHEAT?

"Good morning," Paul said to his supervisor as he reported for his first day of work. "Good morning" she replied. "I must warn you, you are the only man on the crew. If you have a problem working with women, let me know now and not waste each others time," Cindy said. "Oh no," shouted Paul, "women work just as hard as men do and besides, they smell better, too," he added. "Fine," Cindy remarked. "Most guys walk away when they find that they are all alone here," she remarked in disgust.

"Let's go to work then," Cindy ordered.

Paul was new to the island just moving from the north so he took on a landscape job to make extra monies. Already Paul knew very little about plants and flowers for sure but this new tropical variety was very different from anything he had accustomed before.

Cindy had assigned him to weed out the flowerbeds. With his limited knowledge of plant life, he had sadly mistaken the tropical grass and wild flowers for weeds.

"Paul, Paul," Cindy screamed as she ran across the lawn. "What in the world are you doing," she shouted. Paul had pulled out all the flowers that she had planted just days before. He explained his ignorance and then she laughed. She admired his honesty and attitude. "From now on Paul, you work with me," said Cindy. "If I leave you alone, you're going to work me to death," she continued. They smiled at each other and chuckled.

They developed a great working relationship over a period of time. Paul was learning his job well and since they were enjoying each other's company, they continued to work as a team.

Paul thanked and complimented Cindy for allowing him the opportunity to learn a new skill and remaining on the job.

"That's so kind of you Paul," Cindy responded, "My husband never compliments me on anything that I do. He says that this is not a real job." Paul consoled her and ushered in his high admirations for her position and skills. Cindy began giving Paul more responsibilities at work with a much lighter physical duty. Before long, they shared lunch periods together. She also began to bring him treats from her home each time she would cook. "Wow," Paul shouted in delight, "not only are you intelligent and beautiful, but you can cook too. Your husband is a really fortunate man to have you as his wife." "Thanks Paul," Cindy muttered as she walked away with her head down. Suddenly she stopped and turned around. "You really know what to say to make a girl feel good," she said with a smile, "but my husband, well, he's never there. We've rather grown apart. I guess 19 years is a bit too long to be married," she added.

Paul didn't quite know what to say so he finished his lunch in silence, then left. The following days of work, Cindy accented her cosmetic abilities wearing different hairstyles, different perfumes, jewelry, and occasionally a dress.

"How do I look Paul," she questioned him. "Great, beautiful," he said in awe. "If I was your husband we'd be broke," he continued. "Why do you say that," she asked. "Because as good as you look I could never go to work for spending all my time around you," he responded. "Thanks Paul, I really needed to hear that," Cindy cried as she walked over and gave him a kiss. Paul was uncertain as to what to do next. Panicky, he looked around to see if any one saw them. "It's okay Paul; I just wanted you to see what I look like in a dress since you only see me in uniforms all the time."

Paul's body responded as he stood there with a dumbfound look on his face. "You'd better wait here for a while before going back outside," Cindy suggested, "at least until that bulge in your pants go down," she grinned.

After work, Cindy passed Paul as he was headed home. She yelled out to him, "Are you okay, Paul." "No," he answered. "Why, what's wrong," she inquired.

"I can't function now, all I can do is think about you," Paul jested. "Oh, that's so sweet, Paul. Don't you have a girlfriend?" "No, I haven't met anyone here yet," he reluctantly replied. "Here, get in," Cindy said, "let me give you a ride home. I did this to you, the least thing I can do is take care of it for you." Paul agreed and got into the car.

This after work relationship continued for several months. Cindy came over to his house one afternoon and returned his door key. "What's this," Paul questioned in astonishment. "I can't see you anymore," answered Cindy. Paul sat up on the side of the bed. Cindy continued, "I'm falling in love with you, but I can't leave my husband. If he finds out he'll divorce me and after 19 years, there's just too much to lose. We have property, the cars, and a house. I'll have to start all over again. I'm sorry Paul." Then she walked out the door.

BECAUSE OF WOMEN,

Carol and Candy are sisters. They work on the same job, in the same department, only on different shifts. Candy works from 7 am until 3 pm. Carol works from 3 pm until 11 pm. They both lived some 40 miles from their jobs so they car-pool to work and stayed together all day until both shifts were over.

Carol's car broke down one afternoon, so they had no way to get back home. Their friend Bob was just arriving for his shift. He worked from 11 pm until 7 am and he lived only a block from the job.

Carol borrowed his car for the night and returned it the next morning when her sister's shift began. This temporary mishap lasted a little while longer than either one first expected. Never the less, everyone seemed much comfortable with the arrangement. So comfortable, in fact, that Candy started staying over at Bob's house until Carol's shift was done. While she was there, Candy would clean Bob's apartment and cook him food for the following day. Candy and Bob joked around often and while they were at Bob's they pretend to be a married couple. It could only be pretend though because Candy was already married.

One evening while Candy was there, Bob showered as he prepared for work. He and Candy were in a conversation so he left the bathroom door open. He walked out with a towel around him and asked Candy to dry his back and so she agreed. When she was finished she spun him around and saw his large erected groin. She awed and then held it in her hands, and stroked him back and forth.

"Oh girl, let's do this," Bob requested. "No, I can't," replied Candy as she jumped up and left the room. They never spoke on the matter again for the next few days. However, through their body language, one could tell that there was a secret there. Their eye contact was more of an embarrassing glance.

The next afternoon at Bob's: "Listen Carol, we need to talk," Bob began. "I'm sorry about what happened the other day and," Bob continued apologetically before being interrupted. "No need to apologize Bob, I'm sorry too. I wasn't embarrassed about what happened, I just had to go," she offered. "Carol, do you fool around," Bob questioned. "No, but I have," responded Carol. "Do you want to," Bob asked. "Yes," agreed Carol, "but you just can't get me pregnant," she added. "My husband is sterile and then he'll know."

BECAUSE OF WOMEN,

"Good game," said Jackie after losing at chess while visiting with a friend. "Do you want to play again?" she asked. "Sure, why not?" answered Al, "I enjoy beating you anyway," he laughed. "Very funny," she shrugged, "you won't win this time." "It's always so comfortable around your place. I love spending time here with you two. Your house is so warm. This is how a home should be," she said as the game began. "Well, thanks, Jackie. You know you're always welcomed here," replied Al as he prepared to defend his side of the board.

"Snacks anyone?" offered Betty as she entered the room. "Thanks love," Al responded to his wife. "And baby, would you give me another beer too, please." "Okay, and what about you Jackie," answered Betty. "Sounds good, I'll have the same," Jackie replied. "Alright guys, it's getting late for me. I'm about to turn in for the night. I'll see you tomorrow," Betty announced upon her return. "Good night, baby. I'll be in shortly. This is going to be the last game for me," Al said as he kissed Betty goodnight. "Goodnight Betty, and thanks again for everything," Jackie added as she plotted her next move.

"I don't want to say it, but I kind of envy you

two. You guys have everything and you act as if you really care about each other. Check," Jackie said with Betty now in the other room. "We try. Nothing comes easy, all we can do is try," Al said with a sigh. "Good move," he relayed searching to defend his position from an attacking queen.

"Al, can I talk to you about something personal without you thinking badly of me regardless to how you feel about it," asked Jackie continuing to press her attack. "Check," she added. "Of course you can. Who am I to pass judgment, besides, we've been good friends for a long, long time. You can talk to me about anything," he said looking up from the board in need of a more defensive strategy.

"When this game is over, I have to go home," she began. "I hate going home. My husband will be coming home soon and then we'll argue again all night long. We haven't had sex in over a year. I'm horny and I need sex now, and I want you. Checkmate. So what do you think about me now," she asked.

BECAUSE OF WOMEN.

"Don't wait up for me I won't be back until Sunday evening," came the warning from Dorothy as she headed out the door. "Dang, baby, I was kind of hoping that we could have dinner and go dancing this evening," replied Joe. "I'm just going to spend some time with my friends. It's not like you don't see me. I'm here five days a week, so what's the problem," she barked. "No problem love. I thought we were supposed to be working on our relationship. I've been here for three months now and you act like you don't want to be bothered with me," Joe answered. "Look, I don't have time for this right now. My friend Dee-Dee will pick up the kids after school for me and bring them to the house. She's also going to cook some food for you all so you can have hot meals until I get back. We'll talk, I promise. Chow," Dorothy uttered as she left the door.

"Ring, ring," came a sound from the door as evening fell. "Daddy, daddy," shouted the children with joy when Joe opened the door. "Hi, I'm Dee-Dee," the beautiful stranger announced with her hand now extended. "And by the way the kids reacted, you must be Joe," she continued. "Yes, I'm Joe. Dorothy told me that you would be coming. Pleased to meet you," he reciprocated while welcoming her in.

"Well, let's see," she began. "The kids had a great day in school. I took them to the park for a while and bought them ice cream on the way home," as they chattered uncomfortable for some twenty minutes.

"Okay," she said, "I've wasted enough of your time. What do you guys want for dinner?" "I'm not particular," Joe replied. "Whatever you prepare will be fine." "Alright, I must warn you though, I'm heavy handed on the spices," Dee-Dee said. "Great, then we'll get alone just fine. Well, there's the kitchen. Just make yourself at home," he responded now returning his attention to the kids.

"Something smells good in the kitchen," Joe complimented Dee-Dee inhaling the aromas in the air. "Thank you, thank you," she replied. "Here, taste these," she added. "Magnifico'," he responded in delight. "Here, have a seat and I'll fix you and the kids a plate," Dee-Dee insisted. "You don't have to twist my arm," said Joe. "Boys, come and get it," he called out to the kids.

"Okay guys, I'm going now. Hope you enjoy everything. I'll stop by and check on you all tomorrow," Dee-Dee announced while preparing to depart. "Everything is great," complimented Joe. "It has really been a pleasure meeting you," he added as she left.

"Hi guys," Dee-Dee greeted upon her arrival the next evening. I'm off to the gym to play a little basketball. Thought I'd stop by and see if you guys wanted to play," she invited. "You bet," accepted Joe as the kids jumped up and down with joy. "Just give me a minute," he said. "I baked pies last night, so I brought you all one. I also noticed your drinks were low and took the liberty to pick up a six-pack. I hope you don't mind," said Dee-Dee. "Are you kidding? Thanks. Let's go guys," Joe then shouted out to the kids.

"Honey, I'm home," Dorothy yelled when she returned. "Wonder where everyone is," she pondered. "Ahh, apple pie, I see Dee-Dee came through," she said while sampling a slice.

Later that day: "Mommy," the children cheered with glee. "Daddy, mommy's home," they said. "We missed you," stated Joe. "Did you have a good time," he questioned. "What's that supposed to mean," Dorothy responded defensively. "I was out with my friend, that's it," she added. "Nothing baby, just trying to make conversation. Do you feel like talking right now," he asked. "No, I'm tired and need to get some rest for work tomorrow, but we'll talk, I promise. Tell you what, meet me for lunch on Wednesday and we'll talk then," she said. "Fine, we'll talk then," answered Joe.

"Sorry that I've been so distant from you the pass few months," Dorothy began while sharing lunch with Joe. "You know that I love you and I need you in my life. It's just that it's really hard for me to get into a relationship right now. I didn't know how to tell you, but I need some space. I think we should see other people and if we get serious about someone, we'll let each other know first" she explained. "Woman are you crazy," blurted Joe. "Calm down," she said. "Woman, I gave up my job and career to move here and try to keep this family together and you tell me to calm down. Hell, you could have told me this over the phone four months ago, before I got here," he furiously replied. "Well, I've got to go back to work now. We'll talk later. Dee-Dee will be picking up the kids from school and keep them until you close the store. Enjoy your lunch. Chow," were Dorothy's departing words.

"It's been real crazy around here the past year," Joe spoke while talking to Dee-Dee. "You have turned out to be a great friend and a really big help."

"Sometimes I don't know what I'd do without you," he spoke of her in praise. "Actually, I'm making out pretty good," she said. "Dorothy's paying me for child care and you're paying me for homecare. It's like I have a full time job with no boss," she laughed. "But seriously, it's no problem. I rather enjoy it and definitely love the kids. Speaking of Dorothy though, how are you two getting along," she asked. "We're friends with kids together. We hang out sometimes, but I've about given up on her. There are only two things that keep me here. I get to raise my sons and the store that I opened last year is starting to do well now. Otherwise, I'd be history," Joe said emphatically. "I'd better go now, it's gotten really late," Dee-Dee said catching a glimpse at the time. "Well wait, I'll walk you home," offered Joe. "I'm fine. I only live three blocks away," she comforted. "No, it's dark outside and a weekend. You shouldn't be walking the streets by yourself this late. Besides, Dorothy and the kids are out of town for the weekend," he insisted.

"Thanks for walking me home," Dee-Dee said unlocking the door. "No problem, good night," replied Joe. "Oh, I'm sorry," he said apologetic after giving her a kiss. "For what," she exclaimed. "For the kiss. It just seemed so natural," he said. "I know. I expected it to happen a long time ago," agreed Dee-Dee. "But before this goes any further we need to talk and we definitely have to tell Dorothy," she urged.

The following week at the store: "I gave my friends a break tonight to see if you wanted to hang out," asked Dorothy. "Sure, I'm closing up shop in a few minutes," Joe answered. "We need to talk anyway," he said. "Ok, but I have to go to the restroom, come go with me and we can talk in there," she said. "Hey baby, this is kind of kinky. Let's do it right here. We might even get busted. Isn't that exciting," Dorothy said. "Yeah baby, but look, first we need to talk," answered Joe. "You know how you say we should tell each other first before we get serious about someone else. Well, I'm getting serious about someone else," he continued. "Okay, that's cool," she said. "Congratulations, whose the lucky lady," she pondered. "It's Dee-Dee," answered Joe, "we're starting to get kind of close." "What," Dorothy screamed while slapping Joe across the face. "That bitch, she's supposed to be my friend. How could you do something like that to me? I'll kick her butt," uttered Dorothy now storming off to confront Dee-Dee.

PARASITES

A vile unforgiving waste of life with no useful purpose living off some one or something else is a parasite. A foreign entity that attaches itself to a host prey for it's on selfish survival. Once it has sucked the life out of its prey it'll detach itself and move on to another unsuspecting host.

In comparisons, a parasite and relationships have many of the same similarities.

Women in general will seek out a male companion primarily based on his financial aptitude. That will consist of his buying power or his potential to gain buying power. Women don't get dressed up, manicured, and stop by the beauty shop to go out to the park and meet up with a homeless man.

The selection of a host is so vital to the survival of this parasite that the process of selection has created a pecking order in society. The better the order of a man's financial worth and his possessions, the better chance he has of being selected as the next victim.

This woman will come across as fairly intelligent, nice to look at, and as a sensitive and caring being. She'll speak soft and pleasant when she talks to him. She'll laugh at all his little jokes. She'll even wipe the food from his mouth when he eats. At times she will flirt with her eyes and eventually she will make physical contact to certain parts of his body. Whatever it takes to attach herself to a new host she will do.

Eventually this victim will lower his guard as he begins to feel more comfortable around her. He will allow his mind to convince himself that he has found a rare and true treasure here. Believing that she is special and not like the rest he will reciprocate in kind. Now she is attached.

Once attached, she'll smother him with kindness. Sometimes she'll call several times a day just to say, "I'm thinking about you." She'll talk to her friends about how fine he is and how well off he's doing financially. Maybe this person will visit and clean up around his house or prepare a special meal for him when he returns home from work lulling the victim into such a state of relaxation until he doesn't really notice that she's there. Then eventually they'll have sex. Now he's been bitten and the blood will start to flow.

Her drinks will begin to infect this host causing his immune system to weaken thus threatening every fiber of his sole survival. She'll contaminate him in such a way until she becomes a strain on his finances causing pockets and holes in his normal repertoire. It'll eat away at him slowly like the cancerous cells that they are. The wigs that she wore when they first met will be replaced by head scarps. The dinners that she once cooked will become McDonalds or other carry out bags. Then soon the make up and tight jeans that she used to wear will only be seen as she's preparing to head out the door in search of her next victim.

Conversations will change too. Every word of the jokes that she laughed at before will now become scrutinize as if they hold some subliminal type meaning or something. The soft pleasant voice is replaced with the harlequin squeals of a Sci-Fi movie gone badly.

This infectious disease is bold and boastful too. They'll even make songs about their intentions; 'I'm looking for a new love', 'Scrubs', and 'What have you done for me lately'.

Of these warning signs comfort should have been able to be taken for it is the necessary step for the impending detachment. However no comfort can be taken at this time for what should be a welcoming victory. The host is left in a state of a battered, beaten, and bruised individual. Entwined emotions have been damaged in what was once considered an investment into the future. Lost of time and monies squandered will eventually reach a fevered pitch when the tallying is done.

DEADBEAT DADS

Child Support, well at least the letters are right. Actually, it's a politically correct way of saying, 'Crock of Smack'.

The abomination of it all is the fact that it's a failed system and the travesty is that it's allowed to continue.

When a woman talks of child support, she's actually saying, 'Child, I'm supported.' It's just like being a kept woman. Rhetoric would like to say and have you believe that child support is for the intent of the benefit for the child. However, very few children actually feel the benefit of such said support even after it's received. Then again, perhaps the operative word there is '*intent*'.

To sincerely address an issue of unsupported children, one only needs to repeal the child support laws. These laws main purpose is to create jobs for the legal system. Judges, lawyers, probation officers, and jails all benefit more from these laws than any child itself does. Court systems become boggled down with foolishness and wasting valuable taxpayer's dollars. This time and tax dollars could better be utilized elsewhere and even allow the government to downsize.

Child support comes in a variety of forms. It could be a direct payment from the non-custodial spouse, it could be made by payroll deductions, or it could come in the form of a social program. Child support in either form is a substantial economic package that is received by the custodial parent.

Without the guaranteed support of this great economical package, women would be less eager to become pregnant and even less eager to be the custodial parent. This act alone could become a great deterrent in the production of unsupported kids. True, it takes a man and a woman to produce a child. Both parties share equal responsibility to the birth or lack there of, of that child. However, the option of multiple childbirths would not be so attractive if the financial package was removed from the equation. This also could affect parity between the sexes of custodial parents.

Child support also initiates many other sets of problems. It encourages single parent households. No support is received if both parents live together. That would be very unacceptable in a household that encountered normal personal differences, as all households do. Instead of trying to work through differences together like two responsible beings, it makes it much simpler to cash a support check. This is evident in the fact that 2nd and 3rd generations of families are raised through the welfare system.

Under this format, the sole responsibility of the man is to provide finance. While on the woman's part, her support is accepted as basic childcare. That leaves the child, when attended by its mother, vulnerable to her personal animosities and misguided teachings. It also leaves the child a missed opportunity to bond with its father or a males influence. The so called, 'intended benefit' for that child now has been greatly displaced.

It's obscured to suggest that a man is incapable of rearing a child alone or to think that for some reason that a mother is automatically guaranteed to be a better parent.

It promotes discrimination and provides a social base to discourage self-improvement and financial gain.

The support system is based on a percentage of a man's earnings and the number of children involved. A man with one kid and an earnings of $1000.00 a month, pays in the neighborhood of 25% -33% of his salary per month. This relates to $250.00 - $330.00 per month for that child. A man with one child, who earns $3000.00 per month, based on that same formula pays $750.00 - $1000.00 per month. The implication this suggests is that one child is worth more than the other based on earnings. The man earning $3000.00 undoubtedly had to spend a significant amount of money and time in higher education in order to reach that potential without any credit to show for his efforts. This bit of incentive discourages higher education. Child support payments when in order should be based on a flat rate across the board.

Child support encourages fraud. Reporting frauds such as Medicare or tax are often discouraged by the reporting agencies. In a number of cases when the reports are actually made, no action is ever taken against the mother. However, if a delinquency or earning increase is reported by the mother, the authorities will act immediately against the father. If the fathers request a review of his support order, even in writing, then that request mysteriously gets lost or receives a lack of attention for several years.

When child support is received, many mothers immediately rush out to take care of the most important business in the order of priorities. That sometimes includes paying off drug dealers, having their hair done, manicures and nail tips and the wardrobe necessary for that night's very important special occasion. This is one reason why child support payment days are sometimes referred to as 'Mothers Day'. Perhaps on the way back home, the mother will pick up a box of chicken for the kids. That way she won't have to ruin her hair or nails preparing a meal.

If a man fails to pay support he is labeled a 'deadbeat' and is subject to have his licenses suspended, income tax withheld, lottery winnings withheld, earning potential diminished, wages garnished, and possible jail time. If a woman receives support and fails to use it on the kid, nothing is ever mentioned. She receives food stamps, section 8, Medicare, and has the father's case subject to a support increase. She is also allowed to use the kids as a dependent for tax purposes and earn additional monies with earned income credit provisions. The father is denied any dependent claims for tax purposes because the children live in the home with the mother. Keep in mind he is paying for this home. Be it one way or another.

There should be a penalty for multiple child support claims with multiple fathers. If a woman is allowed to use child birth as a means of income then she should also be governed by the laws of a self employed contractor and subjected to pay tax accordingly.

Even for the fortunate few children who actually do benefit from the child support, they grow up with the misguided and misinformed perception that it's because of the child's mother that they have such benefits. The father or non-custodial parent will receive no credit what so ever, for his share of the monies. The child will also benefit from the lies of its mother, such as, 'He doesn't care about you,' or 'He never does anything for you.'

These vicious lies and rumors only stir growth and further the rift of distance between the child and its father.

When the child becomes of adolescence age and that wonderful financial package is near finish, the mother miraculously decides that it's time for the now adult to spend some time with its father and try to form a bond. This miracle takes place because the child becomes a liability and is no longer an asset. If the child gets into trouble on the way to adulthood, then it's suggested that it happened because the child's father was not around or involved in the rearing.

Now, this troubled child ends up in the court system. Once again, the courts become boggled down, wasting valuable time and taxpayers dollars on foolishness. The judges are paid, the lawyers are paid, the probation and jails are paid, and the child, still didn't benefit from the support. It becomes obvious that the system has failed. Then again, 'intent' was the operative word.

APOLOGY TO MY KIDS

It demonstrates a poor quality of character in a
man,
who has not the ability to admit when he is wrong and
for that in which he stands.
It pains me how things happened surrounding this
circumstance,
I had hoped that it would have changed and given us
another chance.

For all the times that I was not there to comfort
you when you pained,
to kiss your boo-boo's, or explain the reasons of the rain,
inside me I know there is no one else to blame,
so here and now for this I will try to explain.

The birthday parties I missed when you were
both three and four,
the Christmas presents you'd see me bringing thru the
front door,
the reasons there were no answers when you wanted to
know more,
know in my heart you kids I'll always adore.

The kite that I never got to teach you to fly,

the times of not being with you that I'd break down and
cry,
the venom mom would spew when she'd call me a lie,
although she would never bothered to explain to you
why.

The way the birds cared for their eggs when we saw
them in their nest,
because I wasn't there didn't mean I loved you any less,
but unlike those birds we created such an ugly mess,
that in the interest of you kids we thought this would be
best.

No compensation would be enough in anything that I say
or do,
nor would it replace the love and joy that comes with
you.
I'm guilty of making bad decisions in some of the things
that I did,
like choosing your mother when I decided to have kids.

MUSTA BEEN CRAZY
(to sleep with   your mama)

"Oh, crap, what did I do last night? This is one of the reasons I shouldn't drink, everything looks good." Paul rambled in his head. He couldn't remember if it was because of her that he needed a drink or because of the drink that he needed her. Whatever it was, he knew that he needed a drink now. "I'd better get up and out of here before she awakes." Paul thought as he reached for his clothes. "Darn, didn't make it. Another of her enlightening conversations is just what I need to start the day."

"You're no good, you're lazy." "I hate the day I met you." "You're going to take care of these kids, and you're going to keep paying these bills." "Why don't you just leave?" Grace continued as she greeted Paul with a verbal assault.

This abusive tongue-lashing must have gone on for at least an hour.

When she finally became exhausted from listening to herself talk and things quieted down Paul said, "Good morning to you too, dear."

This infuriated Grace deeply. It suddenly reminded her of a few more choice ideas she held in her heart for the man that she once loved enough to father

her kids.

Her tone and antics thru the bickering lit a kinder spirit with Paul. This caused him to chuckle as he found great humor in this chain of events. Already he knew the outcome of this entire scenario.

Repeatedly they had relived the scenes of this 'off again, on again' relationship. This time was just to be one more link in their chain. Only difference, this time Paul found himself at wits end and had permanent plans on finalizing his departure.

"Yeah, right. I knew you'd come through with that one eventually. Every time I pay the bills and spend my money, you start that same old stuff," Paul replied. "It makes no sense to keep going through this. People shouldn't have to live like this. This thing is over, one way or the other. I'll be back to get my things later," Paul added. "Good, take your butt on loser. You ain't getting crap out of here," Grace snapped back.

Paul tried several times unsuccessfully to retrieve his possessions. Each time Grace would meet him with relentless grief. Neighbors tired of being subjected to this family squabble once again called the police.

"Look, you two," said Officer Mahoney upon his arrival to the scene. "We are exhausting a lot of resources and manpower with you two. Your case has to be settled in civil court, and Paul, if you're caught around here before that time, then you will be arrested." Paul retreated disgusted and frustrated, but not before Grace was able to get in one final jab. "Loser, loser," she taunted as he exited the driveway.

About a month later their court date had arrived. Paul found no particular joy of seeing Grace again. He was however, delighted about a chance to see his kids. Even if this chance to see them was only in court.

Somehow, it seemed quite pointless. He knew that he'd never truly have her removed from his life because of the kids. However, because of the kids, he felt that this breakup had to be done. The recent years had been too much strain on the children. They had to watch the two people that they love, argue and fight all the time.

Paul was uncertain as to what the outcome of the case might be. He felt though, that he had a convincing and compelling case. Regardless of the results, this chapter in their life, he knew, must end.

"All rise," the bailiff announced as the judge entered the room. Then silence fell and the presence of tension and apprehension hung stagnating through out the air. After a few procedures, the bailiff would continue. "Your honor, this is case number 9876 on the docket; Paul Another-man verse Grace Any-witch."

Paul came prepared as he began to plead his case. His possessions contained bank statements, check stubs, receipts, and notarized documents. His attire was casual and his presentation eloquent.

Grace came armed with four kids. Two of which were Paul's and two borrowed from a neighbor next door. She also had in her possession a bottle of crocodile tears that she could turn off and on at will.

Paul pleaded his case. Grace interrupted several times without acknowledgement from the judge. She often brought out the crocodile tears, and later accompanied them with an occasional fainting spell.

"That's quiet all right, Ms. Any-witch," the judge would say. Silence fell over Paul, as by now, he could predetermine the progression of this case. Each party fired a few more salvoes. Grace took a whiff of the stench in the air. She could sense that she was losing.

Grace stringently fought back, "and your honor, he has never paid any child support."

Paul made a menacing glare at the judge. At this point, they made eye contact. Paul figured, "no way in the hell he's going for that stuff, I've got proof." Paul had seen this stunt too many times before, besides, they lived together. Suddenly, Grace fell to the floor again with more instant tears.

"I've heard enough of this case," roared the

judge. "I rule in favor of the defendant, she gets to keep everything for the benefit of the kids." "Fine," Paul said as he exited the room.

Grace jeered at him one more time on departure, "Loser, loser, loo…ser" "That's enough, Ms. Any-witch," said the bailiff.

Paul moved away and left Grace in the home which he had been purchasing. He saw no reason to continue spending money just to have it taken away. Grace moved away and left the home in foreclosure. Paul was now in jeopardy of losing his entire investment.

He found himself now in further debt in an effort to save his home. Grace was hysteric to learn that Paul had reoccupied the home. Three days later, she filed for child support and furthered Paul's financial woes.

Several years passed without any contact from Grace. Paul had only limited encounters to spend time with his kids. Grace often relocated from state to state making visitation attempts that much more difficult.

During one of his efforts to visit his kids, Paul was involved in an auto collision. The results were devastating. He was now a quadriplegic and his financial applecart was in total disarray.

Paul's hefty child support payments had now been reduced to mere social security awards. This forced

Grace to return to work. Unfortunately, Paul lost everything. He lost his house, car, job, family, and friends. During the next three years, Paul made great strides in his recovery. Grace, however, was now finding life difficult without the benefit of that check. She now decided that she no longer wanted to be a mom. Three years had gone by without a word from her and now this.

The phone ranged. It was Grace on the other side of the receiver. "Hi honey, how are you," came the recognizable voice. "I just called to see how you were doing." Torn between rage and elation, Paul said nothing. "Hey baby, are you there," the chilling voice asked. "So to what do I owe this honor," he replied. "I was just thinking about you. I know it's been a while since we talked and the kids want to see you again," she added. He knew from previous experience with her that this was a bad idea. He also knew that a chance to be with his kids again was worth any risk.

She had been through a change of instability over the pass three years and now needed a place to live. Paul agreed to allow them to stay for the good of the kids. Besides, in his now diminished state of health, he could use some assistance. They agreed to get together upon a Labor Day weekend. It would be a perfect arrangement. It was the last summer holiday and an opportunity for the kids to settle down before the school year restarted.

Two days before the holiday, Paul received another call. "Hey baby," came again her voice. "I'm having trouble with the car and it's going to take me a couple days to get it repaired. I'm going to send the kids on down and I'll be there as soon as it's done. Okay?"

He found himself in a non-negotiable position.

Something smelled like a rat, but if it were true, then the kids would have waited by the side of the road. "Okay, what time should I meet them," he said.

The holiday had come and gone. The kids were now in school. Grace was nowhere to be found. The kids each only had a couple of change of clothes and all needed new wardrobes now that winter was approaching. Six months had passed before Paul received another call. "Hey baby," came the voice on the other side of the phone. "I'm sorry baby, but I've been through all kinds of changes since I last talked to you." "No kidding," He replied, "me too." "I know that you're mad at me right now baby, but I need a place to stay for a while," pleaded Grace. "I'm sorry Grace I can't help you right now. I needed some help during my times too and my friend helped me with the kids. Since then, we've gotten married and I can't do her like that. Wish I could help you right now but I just can't. Sorry Grace," Paul relayed.

"That's okay," Grace said. "The social security is about to run out anyway, and besides, the kids ain't your children. Looser, looser, loo…ser," she jeered at him one last time.

DEAR DIARY

During the days house cleaning lay this book that fell to the floor when the sheets were removed from the bed. At first it seemed like no big deal. Just pick it up and place it on the nightstand. When the dusting began, it became necessary to move this book again. This time however, it landed on the reverse side. The title of the book became visible. It read; 'DIARY.'

Later that day when the workload subsided, interested peaked, and curiosity mounted. Looking inside this book entered the imagination. It never should have happened, but it did. Once inside, this is some of what was found:

Dear Diary,

Today I am mad at my mom. She did not pick me up again today. She always says she is going to do something and never does. I think grown people should do what they say.

Dear Diary,

Today was not a good day. I have not been to school for two weeks now because I don't have shoes or a coat to wear. I miss my friends. People should not have children if they cannot take care of them. My children will not have to live like I do.

Dear Diary,

I love my mom but sometimes she makes me sad. Every time I call her she is never there. She is a good mom until she gets around her new boyfriend. I am not going to call her again until she calls me first.

Dear Diary,

I am kind of excited today. Today I am going to go and live with my dad. We have not been able to spend a lot of time together since I was a little kid. I don't know what to expect but I am looking forward to learning to do things a different way.

Dear Diary,

It's different here at my dads. I have my own room and the biggest bedroom in the house. I like my new school. The kids here talk funny but everyone is nice to me. My dad is strange. He helps me with my homework.

WOMEN'S RECEIPT

For an award-winning recipe that is sure to please the palate and turn out successful every time, just follow these simple instructions and you too can be like the pros.

First, start with the complete truth. Then cut into several pieces, using only those pieces of your selective choice.

Next, marinate overnight in rumors, lies, and conversations with friends, family, and loved ones.

Add in four quarts of bullshit and bring to a boil.

Serve under your own agenda using crocodile tears and season to taste.

Eureka, you have successfully completed an entrée that will be satisfying to the soul.

LIARS TALK

"Liars talk, and fools like me believe," a song
once began, but the prevalence of those words never
became more apparent until adulthood was achieved. It
is found that in relationships women often begin there
lies with things as simple as their age, their hair color, or
their sexual history. Women will lie about their shoe size
and the size dress that they wear. They will lie about
their previous life-style or their rates of infidelity. A
woman will lie about how good of a person she has
been, knowing all the time that she is full of tricks and
games.

Women will tell you how committed they are in
having a good working relationship or perhaps how
horrible of a person their partner was in a pervious
ordeal. They may have even experienced multiple
partners in their life, but will come away from each
situation with the same conclusion, 'a good man is hard
to find', or 'all men are dawgs.'

A woman will lie about whether or not she is
pregnant sometimes in an attempt to get a man to stay.
She will lie about having an abortion or how many she
has had. They will lie about their ability to conceive a
child. The *'mauther'* of all the lies though, is the one that
she'll tell you about whether or not the child is yours.

She will lie to her own child, convincing them that she is always right and would never lie to them while knowing all the time that she is telling them a lie.

She will lie to them about how hard she works to take care of them, even though the support checks are coming in from somewhere else. And women love to lie about their finances, while conveniently failing to mention the food stamps or government assisted living that she is receiving. Without hesitation though, she'll tell the kids how deadbeat and no-good their fathers are although she'll fail to bring up all the accounts that she has open using the children's names.

Women will tell you how their mate ignores them and takes them for granite while she is laying up in the arms of another man for comfort and pleasure.

Sadly enough though, eventually they'll tell you how they have been used and abused by men. But, of course, now you know that that's just another one of the things that she will lie about, too.

'ODE TO A BITCH I KNOW'

Is it half man or is it half beast,
No one can really tell for sure.
One thing that I do know,
A makeover wouldn't be the cure.

Never does a thing that's wrong,
Self professed to always be right,
According to her, she made the heavens and
Then she made the light.

She's perfect form in every way
To that she will attest,
But, if this is meant for perfection;
Then boy, what a hell-u-va mess.

She often questions her own gender,
When she's loud and misbehaves,
But soon she'll calm right down,
Once she's had a shave.

Mad at the world for what the God's did,
Kept her pregnant so she'd stay hide.
Nobody finds her attractive 'because she has no class,
As far as man's concerned, she's just a piece of ass.

So since you have no worthy purpose in life,

And your everyday is consumed with grief and strife,

I offer these words to bid you well,

Better yet, why don't you just go to hell!

STEP UP TO THE PLATE

'Step up to the plate', words of wisdom that have become the new catch phrase of the millennium. This is an often used baseball term that has found its way into mainstream everyday social usage. In baseball it signifies 'the beginning of a performance' or 'making an attempt to execute an act'. Socially, however, it refers to 'taking control of' or 'assuming responsibility for'.

Well, in either case, one must first understand and appreciate the act itself in order to enjoy the correlations between the two. One first approaches the plate unassumingly and unable to predict the outcome of the task in which they are about to partake. Armed only with enthusiasm and anticipation this person takes a stance and digs in for the inevitable regardless of the results.

While at the plate, this person has three attempts at a minimum to offer up their best performance. From this seemingly effortless position lies a multitude of options and paths, many of which, one has no control.

The result of these options comes in three main categories. These categories are: 1. on base, 2. out, and 3. Score. Each category further divides again into a long list of other options.

Plainly, everyone's desired goal is to score.

However, rationally, that goal will seldom be achieved. In as much, this transformation carries over to everyday life.

Understandably, baseball is just a game, but living has also been referred to as the game of life.

When one examines life situations, that same unassuming and unpredictable outcome is present. Individuals involved are armed with the anticipation and enthusiasm for the inevitable. Once again, the consequences hold little or no regard. Naturally, everyone 'steps up to the plate' with the intentions of offering up their best performance or to score. As in baseball, this position too, offers a multitude of options and paths. Many of these paths also, will offer little or no control, only chance.

These options fall into different categories too. These categories are: 1. Survival, 2. Failure, and 3. Success, each featuring a list of circumstances to achieve a particular goal.

Not everyone will be successful, even though that is the intended desire.

Therefore, now that perchance you have a clearer understanding of the actual event itself, then your participation will be much wiser. Just because it is cute, popular, or fanatic to offer up the catch phrase 'step up to the plate', please keep in mind that this comfort offers no guaranteed success.

Here-in is where the similarities between baseball and social usage end. Socially this phrase primary use is to implicate the solicitation of financial support from the father of a child. As by all rights, the father should be held accountable for sharing in the support and rearing of a child. After all, this is part of the responsibility for 'attempting to execute an act', regardless of the inevitable consequences. Unfortunately though, this phrase has another implication. It implies blame or guilt. Basically, it uses a man as a scapegoat. It insinuates a man is irresponsibility. Actually, there is a great bit of irresponsibility involved here, however, it begins way before it reaches this point.

'Stepping up to the plate', includes practicing in abstinence or sharing in safe sex. It consists of the use of birth control and exercising family planning. 'Stepping up to the plate' also require one to make better choices when choosing a mate. As far as irresponsibility's goes, that would include childbirth out of wedlock, birthing multiple children with multiple partners, and birthing children when you're not even sure who the father is. It's pretty irresponsible to birth a child without first having provided a nurturing family setting or financial provisions for that child.

Just for the sake of argument, let us assume that

it's true; a man will sleep with anything. Let us also assume that it's true, that men are 'dawgs'. Well, short of rape, there is no way in hell a man can have sex with a woman long enough to impregnate her unless she is irresponsible too. There's a saying that goes: 'If you sleep with dogs, then expect to get fleas', so ladies, stop being irresponsible and 'step up to the plate'.

CHILD SUPPORT the RETIREMENT PLAN

"This is a great unforgettable occasion as I write this check," Chuck exclaimed with gleam in his face. "A day I never thought I'd see," sealing the envelope and waving it in the air. Then he poured himself a drink as he and his friend celebrated in song and dance.

"Don't think I've ever seen anyone that happy before when they're paying bills. It never worked for me anyway," his friend Denise, remarked. "So what's the reason," she asked.

"Ahh baby, just let me tell you. Twenty-four years ago when I was just a young man, I though I knew it all," he began reminiscing as he told his story. "When I was out sowing my oats I met this girl and it was like love at first sight. People say that all the time, well it was no different for me either. However, at nineteen we knew it all and no one could tell us otherwise.

Therefore, we fooled around and played house. Did all the things that grown folk do and had a good time at it too. A year or so down the line things started to get real serious so we decided to get married. A dream comes true, now with the love of my life 'til death do us part'. Who could have asked for anymore?

We had a kid and a promising future. We worked together on a part-time business that we started together and had plans of retiring at thirty-five years of age. Then two years later we had another child," he said, stopping to refresh his drink.

"Well, at this point things started to boggle down. Reality sat in, this was our future together."

"Unfortunately though, we began to grow up, realizing all the things that we did not know. We wondered about all the things that we did not do. We even wished for all the places that we did not see. An uneasy spirit hovered over the air of love like a low fog to the ground and tensions started to flare.

It started out as little things. She'd leave the cap off the toothpaste. I'd be late picking her up from work. She'd overspend the budget. I'd eat the last piece of pie. Just stupidity, excuses are what they were. I think we both kind of had the same feelings but neither knew how to talk to each other about it without being the bad guy.

Big mistake! Because we couldn't communicate our feelings to each other all the tension stayed bottled up inside. Cheery, loving conversations soon became short and snappy ones. Next, pointing the fingers of blame and name-calling began. Any kind of an excuse would do. All the time that we cherished together was replaced by spending it apart. What a mess we had made of it all. No one was really trying anymore.

It was crazy as hell, I tell you. It wasn't like we

didn't care about each other. It wasn't like we weren't in love. We both loved our kids and wanted the best for them. Seemingly, though, we had different opinions of what the best was and how to go about getting it for the kids that we loved. All of our young adult life had been about just us. Now all of our future was going to be about just us. We didn't even know who we were ourselves individually. Knowing what I know today though, I think the truth of the matter is that we both wanted it to part," Chuck said as he paused and walked to the patio for a breath of fresh air.

He continued when he returned, "We didn't have enough experience to know how to fix our problems. Although, I doubt at this point it would have made much difference anyway. Therefore, we parted. Funny thing though, after we parted jealousies sat in. We weren't even able to remain friends. That's when we divorced. She moved to New York and me, well, I stayed here.

Naturally, she got the kids and I got to write the checks. I've been writing them checks for twenty years now. It's been rough sometimes, but you do what you've got to do. Hell, I've juggled bills, had my lights cut off, and on occasion ate just rice for a week in a row in between paychecks.

Okay, so I didn't quiet get to retire at thirty-four.

After all, it was just a goal. When you think about it though, forty-three is not bad either. Man! This feels good. Yesterday I retired from twenty years on the job, my house is now paid for, and this month my baby graduates from college. You have no idea how good this feels. It's like hitting the lottery. All this time I've gotten use to living without that money and now it's here. Mine, all mines," Chuck finished with glee. "Wow! Congratulations. Now I understand your joy," Denise said.

"It couldn't have worked out any better if I had planned it. Cheers!" he toasted to Denise again in a celebratory dance.

A GENTLE MAN

There was a time in my life when I couldn't stand the man. The defenseless way he'd cowardly run from my mom when she'd be in one of her bitter fits of rage. These were a couple of the thoughts that passed thru my mind as I sat there in disbelief. Luther Vandross's song, 'Dance with my father again', was playing softly in the background. One by one, another speaker would take their turn at the altar. Each speaking praise so highly and eloquent of someone they've loved, cherished, and come to know.

Co-workers, neighbors, and friends were reading and speaking from documents where their words had been chosen so carefully. He'd lie there with a seemingly smile on his face from some of the jokes that were being told on his behalf. One could have only tried to imagine what would have been on his mind. An orchestrated crescendo of highs and lows would range thru out the program. There were the highs of laughter of the jokes being told to the lows of tears when a more solemn mood would be spoken. Instantly my mind was called back to a time when we worked the same job together. The pride he displayed. I remembered the statuette way he would stick out his chest. That boastful grin on his face, and that utterly bit of surprise, as he was unaware that I would introduce him as my dad. He swaggered when he walked. A priceless moment this was for sure.

I remembered as a child when we'd enjoy peaches and ice cream after Sunday's dinner. Peaches that he'd prepared in his own special way and ice cream that he had churned by hand. My sisters and I would look forward to him coming home from work on the weekends for he'd always be bearing gifts. Gifts of nothing more than trinkets as I look back on it now, but it were mainly the thoughts that really mattered.

Sometimes he would amuse us by doing his two-hand headstands then walking up and down the stairs. I remembered some of the special cuisines that he would prepare with the leftovers from the Thanksgiving dinners. One in particular he'd call 'Mulligan Stew'.

Even some forty years later, regardless of where we were, we'd travel for miles just to be near each time that he would barbeque. The time and preparations he would take to make his sauce. The artistic way he would maneuver between the outdoor grill and the kitchen.

There would be the aroma in the air that could be smelled from seemingly miles around. Not to mention the festive atmosphere it would create with large gatherings of friends, family, and neighbors as they each waited impatiently for their chance to sample his wares.

Next, the great grandchildren took their turns displaying their love and admiration to someone they held so dear. Everyone had their own special little story or memory that they wanted to share. Their numbers were fifteen in all. Their parents and his grandkids would follow them. Their numbers would reach sixteen.

It was funny how many times the stories of his barbeque sauce and secret recipes were reiterated. Others highlighted the strength of his work ethics. Many spoke of his character and the way he genuinely gave and shared in love. They even spoke of his shy smile and his 'Santa Claus' type belly. Tears were still a flow, but as each speaker fought through the tears the strength in their voice would only grow. A smile would show on their face with the strength of conviction that the gifts of life which he had given them could never be taken away.

Their parents followed the grandchildren. They would be the remaining four of his five children. There was not really much more that could be said in his behalf at this point that the people here didn't already know. It more at this point served as a personal forum for everyone to express their emotions and personally say good-bye.

Then it was my turn. Last but not least. I was not last because of the order of my birth, but because of the order that I had chosen. Now I represented the senior male figure of the family and it was my chosen desire to close.

Slowly heading to the altar I passed him by to take one final glimpse and to say goodbye. Everything that I wanted to say had already been said. So there in silence stood I with teary eyes while listening to the hymns that played. Nothing new seemed to come to my mind. My silence however seemed to have captivated the audience and commanded their undivided attention. Everyone by now was curious as to what I had to say. When I looked over the multitudes in the crowds it all became very clear. Everything they said had been oh so true. A couple of things though they did fail to mention. With all the things that he had done and said, he was often under appreciated and occasionally taken for granted because of his kind heart.

Nevertheless, foremost and all what was the most important and impressive thing to me was the way he command this much presence. A packed room filled with hundreds of people inside. Speakers singing praise to the point that the entire program itself extended by a couple of hours. The legacy that he left behind will definitely be a hard pair of shoes to fill. I realized that not only was he a great man, but I had lost a father and most of all, I had lost a friend. It occurred to me that everyone felt in their own way that they had an idea of which this man was when no one even had a clue. Even though he had been a father to us all, he didn't have a child in the entire room. In his lifetime, he never had kids of his own. He married this woman, my mom, a woman with five kids already. He raised us all equally as his own. This family grew to what it is today through his hands and guidance. This fact has rarely ever been mentioned. In our hearts, minds, and souls, he will always be 'Dad'.

WHAT THE FUNK?

Jerry Springer, Maury Povich, Montel Williams, just to name a few. Getting paid, made a living off bull that you know ain't true.

Better than penicillin, better than canned beer, even better than sex itself. One of the best things that has been discovered in mans existence is the use of DNA.

Here you stand, 'holier-than-thou', looking down your nose at me. Talking bad about me to everyone you meet. Criticizing the things that I do, and blaming me for the things that I don't.

There was once in time when all a woman had to do was go take a trip downtown and take out a warrant for non-support. The rest was history. Your butt was grass. The local sheriff would show up at your house or job armed with a warrant and serves you right there on the spot if they didn't lock you up. If you ever had sex with that woman, it was now your baby, whether it was yours or not.

Can you imagine how many men have taken care of babies that weren't theirs just because some woman said so? Heaven forbid if you happened to be an attractive looking man or a financial stable man. It was like walking around with a bulls-eye on your back.

Next you would get the dubious honor to present

yourself in front of some sanctimonious self-serving judge. The entire situation would literally be a joke to him. He'd assess you a monthly dollar value backed up with the threat of jail time and their snide bits of wisdom; "If you feed the baby long enough then it'll look just like you." Old folk used to say, "Mama's baby, daddy's maybe."

"Take care of that baby. Be a man," the world would shout out instructively. What a joke. It was a green light to lie being confirmed. Men had to live with this horror. Can you imagine that?

Some people would tell tales of how their parents had been together some 50, 60, or 70 years. Like that was suppose to be impressive or something. That's probably just to minimize the fact of infidelity. Better yet, an attempt to shame one into humiliation to stay in a relationship. However, if the truth be told, people tiptoed behind the barns and in the hay field's years ago, too. Infidelity is probably just as old as sex. That's why everyone's family has one of those relatives that don't quite favor the rest of the mix or has something distinguishingly different about them. Family members always seemed to be able to explain away some of those differences though. 'You've got a head like Uncle Bob.' 'She took after her great grandmother," they would all say. People had excuses that were equally as available as the number of illegitimate kids back in the days. This in many cases would resurface that old story of 'God gave me this baby'.

Next came a period when men would dare stand up for themselves and challenge the legitimacy. Well low and behold, up would pop out the new label makers of our time. 'Dead Beat Dads'. The television shows and the public cried out in outrage.

Male bashing was at an all time high. Manhood had a new challenge. He would have to be the scum of the earth. For no real man would deny or challenge the legitimacy of a cute little baby, now would he? Child support groups sprung up like trees in the wilderness. Men were humiliated in courts and on television shows across the land. Payroll checks suffered automatic deductions. Tax refunds were confiscated. Credits would be denied. Licenses were suspended and properties were levied. Even the conservative TV shows began to switch formats just to be able to jump in on the bandwagon. Heck, in some cases you could even get your picture plastered across the local newspaper.

This controversy has existed at least all the way back to 'Joseph and Mary'. It existed so long, in fact, that it became the norm and an acceptable part of life. Then along came a wise man. Disguised in the cloak of a scientist, he was able to break the code of DNA. With the key to genetic material now at his disposal, he was able to prove definitively and irrefutably, beyond the shadow of a reasonable doubt, the relationship between the two people involved. The irony of it all though is the fact that it is accepted proof in legal and social circles around the world. It turned out to be a great tool and marketing strategy for the courts and TV show ratings. The label makers rushed in again, 'step up to the plate', they urged.

Today's shows feature the same type of scenario with the same type host of characters. There is however, a slight new added twist. After the suspected father has been introduced and once again belittled, booed, betrayed and humiliated, the result of the test comes out. The mothers are jeering, "Yeah, bring it on, bring it on," they say. They threaten to take him to court for child support. Even her mother is there all in the man's face.

The envelope is opened and the document is removed. The reading of the paper goes, "the result of the test is 99.9% positive that you are *not* the father of this child." "Boo-hoo-hoo," the mother moans. Then the 'crocodile' tears start to flow as she is consoled by the host and the crowds. The host and audience concerned now only with the welfare of the child, leave the innocent man totally ignored. No I'm sorry. No I was wrong. No here's your money back. No nothing. All this innocent man receives for his erroneous humiliation is a hurried exit off the stage. Still the host will make one last cynical remark basically saying; "you dodged a bullet that time, you lucky bastard."

Here's the good part. The tragedy of the story shifts. Everyone's concern is for the fatherless child. As a truly concerned individual and good talk show host, they offer their services again to try and find the father of this child. Another man is about to take the walk of shame. The excitement of the show comes when man after man is accused and led to slaughter just to find that the results again are the same. They are *not* the fathers of this child. Alas, a father is identified, the couple reconciles, and the story ends happy.

Years ago, innocent men would have had their lives ruined taking care of someone else kids while the mother knew all the time that she had not been true in their relationship.

Some stories get even better than this. Some women have this man whom they make claims of loving. He's made a good home for her and their kid. Now the kid is about four, five, or six years old and she decides that she needs to tell him something. Big surprise! She tells him that the child may not be his.

Each woman on stage seeking to prove the paternity of her child involves anywhere from three, five, and up to eight different men. Each one of these men, who dare challenge or question the paternity are referred to as 'dawgs'. The question is how is it that a woman can have sex with so many men at one time that she doesn't even know who the true father is? If this challenge he questions makes a man a 'dawg', then what does that have to say about the woman who needs to tell her children that she slept around?

This part of the story, however, always seems to get swept under the rug. So, 'what the funk?'

9 MONTHS/ 18 YEARS

"I carried you for nine months," an irate mother was overheard saying while scolding her disobedient child. Immediately came to mind was the story of 'Footprints in the Sand.'

In this story, a wearied traveler at the end of a trying journey looks back over his triumphs and he notices only one set of footprints. In his talk with God he questions Him. "Lord," he said, "I thought you said that you'd be there for me." "I thought you said that you would be there every step of the way, but all I see here is one set of footprints in the sand."

God answered in reply, "Yes, I was there for you, and the reason you see only one set of footprints is because I carried you every step of the way."

Just like the traveler, mothers tend to highlight the significance of their role in child rearing while overshadowing the contributions of others.

It then came to realization that in every three year cycle four 9 month intervals will have passed. There are six three year cycles in a child's life before that child reaches 18 years of age. This is important because 18 years is how long a father is responsible for contributing into the raising of that child. Over that 18 year period, twenty-four 9 month intervals will occur.

Easily both sides could state equal debatable cases in an attempt to hyphen or justify there positions. However, the gravity for the bases of a success can not be out-weighed by the mere completion of an act itself.

Even if one considers with punitive, as many will, the positions of single parent households where the mother is predominately the custodial parent, she still receives more credit, sympathy, and exposure than she is truly deserving. This is not a case of making light of a mother's contributions but more over a case for strengthening those contributions made by a man.

One must be made to understand that the single parent household is merely an illusion. It exists in appearance only. The majority of the benefits that household will receive are due to contributions of the father, whether directly or indirectly. Even in situations where the fathers contributions are made directly to the household that house will still receive outside support at the expense of the father.

It's ludicrous to suggest that a father is not contributing because of the government housing and subsidies one might receive such as food stamps, Medicaid, etc. For every service provided will surely be repaid by that father in one form or another be it child support to the state, license and tax lost, or simply jail time.

So just like that traveler, one might not appreciate the journey they had to take to get down to the end of the road, but it definitely doesn't mean they didn't have help along the way.

Therefore, in hindsight, a 9 month maternity period is essentially a very small price to pay.

THE TRUTH HURTS

Okay ladies, so as much as it pains me to say, I must whole-heartily agree, 'men are dawgs.' Oddly enough though, in order to root out the problem, one must identify the source and place the responsibility squarely on the shoulders of where it deserves to be.

In life's story women often have the tendency to criticize men and find fault in the things that they do. They find men unworthy of their time and compassion. They find men as cheaters and incapable of love. When in realty, men are just what women will them to be.

You see, most male kids are raised in single households, where mom is the deciding factor in their growth. From the 'cradle to the grave', men learn everything that they know about women, from women and their influences. That includes the lying, cunning, deception, manipulation, cheating, and the rest of the lot.

Sure, it has to be very difficult to find traits and characteristics in a man that you absolutely despise. In fact, it must be like seeing your own reflection in a mirror with a big pimple on your nose. Obviously, these matters create problems in relationships and commitments with each other. That's the real tragedy of the story. Fret not though, you can still find some solace in the situation, in as much as you've taught men well. The hard lesson that you fail to learn though, is that **'man'**, is not defined by **'wo-man.'** A man's worth is not measured by how he falls, but how he gets back up.

If you figure that men are dawgs, then you shouldn't be surprised at what they do. Through your hard work of grooming, training, and handling, you have gotten just what you wanted, a 'man'. If you think he's a dawg, then leave the dawg alone.

However, the solution to the problem seems very clear and simple. If you really want men to stop acting like dawgs, then stop treating them like one and ***'take off the leash.'***